Travelling Through Time

Travelling Through Time

Carston Warner

gatekeeper press™
Columbus, Ohio

Traveling Through Time

Published by Gatekeeper Press
2167 Stringtown Rd, Suite 109
Columbus, OH 43123-2989
www.GatekeeperPress.com

The cover design for this book is entirely the product of the author. Gatekeeper Press did not participate in and is not responsible for any aspect of this element.

ISBN (paperback): 9781662913037

eISBN: 9781662913044

ACKNOWLEDGMENTS

I would like to thank my daughter Caron, who was very supportive in helping me to compile this collection of poems, as well as supporting me with navigating the world of creativity, which included attending various writing groups and providing positive feedback.

I would also like to thank my daughter Marisa and my son Matt for providing some valuable feedback.

I have a host of friends, coworkers, therapists, Meeting Group members, and others who provided various materials and knowledge that fueled my creative juices. Most of all, they were and are there when I need them.

I have three sisters and one brother remaining from a family of nine siblings—Lucy, Rose, Sherman, and Marion. At some point in life, we all shared the same space, but not always at the same time. It is important for me to mention them because they all played a key role in my youth as well as in my development over time, especially my siblings who are no longer with me—Joe, "Sister" Elizabeth, John, and Dave.

Last but not least, I would like to thank my wife Jean, who stayed on the roller coaster of life and time with me. She was and is always there to help me find that balance of sorting information that may have been perceived as challenging at times but panned out to be less complicated than perceived. Over many years of "Traveling Through Time" in our relationship, in our marriage, and raising children, we have overcome barriers, obstacles, and challenges. Thanks for staying with me.

CONTENTS

Soldier In Vietnam

I think of Vietnam day and night.
God only knows how many GIs have lost their life.

They fight by day.
They fight by night,
not knowing who is next to lose their life.

Dreams of peace enter their minds
whenever they have some priceless time.

Sometimes they pray when the going gets rough.
They can't wait for an answer.
They have to prove they are tough.

BOOM!   BOOM!   BOOM!
ROCKETS EXPLODE ALL AROUND!!!

I cover my head.
Pretend I'm dead.
Open my eyes.
Come back alive.

My buddy has gone to the heavens above.
I hope he finds peace,
most of all, love.

Sometimes I think he is more fortunate than I.

He has gone home to rest.

I am still a damn GI.

I am tired of fighting this never-ending war.

I don't even know what I am fighting for.

My minister told me when I was a boy,

"THOU SHALT NOT KILL!
THIS GUN ISN'T A TOY!"

Help me, Father, to obey your law.

Help me understand what I am fighting for.

If I lay my gun aside,

will you be my savior and guide?

Take me to heaven so that I can forget

all of the things I have seen

In which, someday, I will regret.

The soldier laid his gun aside and walked into the mist of the eerie morning silence...In the distance you could hear an automatic weapon's rapid fire...A stiff, still quietness came over the battlefield. A slight breeze brushed past me...I can still hear the voice of the praying GI...

Thank you, Father, for answering my prayer.

The pains in my mind, I could no longer bear.

I am more fortunate than a lot of GIs,

who return home to lead troubled lives...

Malcolm

Systematically uneducated
because of
inadequate facilities
faulty by
color and context.

K – K – K
instilled fear
and cursed by the adjective
Black,
a revolutionist was born.
A messiah,
a god
in a deep tomb of darkness,
who
educated himself behind bars,
in bars,
small streaks of light
resembled a grid pattern of life.
The messiah's reign declined in bars;
behind bars
he flourished.
The streaks of light grew larger
as the sun rose higher
and higher.

From the deep tomb of darkness, a shadow appeared
disdained,

stained, and labeled pimp, pusher, hustler.

"Big Red"

a prisoner.

"We should unite on the one thing
we all have in common!" he cried.

His cry was heard in Watts, Chicago, Harlem.

"The one thing we all have in common,"

the voice rang and rang

in Mississippi,

Georgia,

and Alabama.

He was labeled a revolutionist

to die a militant's death.

Struck by assassin's bullets,

for what?

Uniting people for what they have in common

and unsystematically educating himself.

A General With a Dream Without a Gun

His dream started deep in the south
when a middle-aged Black woman refused to move out.
This Black woman's most vigorous lust
was to take a seat in the front of the bus.

"Mr. Charlie," southern policemen were called then,
thought this woman had committed a sin.
They called in the law, which was mostly unjust.
Police appeared on the scene and made an arrest.

Then came the boycotts and many other sins;
here is where the general, still unknown, begins.
A man of strength, courage, and steel.
A peace-loving man, spreading goodwill.
A warrior, a general who never would kill,
even though he led many armies over the hills.

Beaten, tortured, dragged in the streets,
a non-fighting general, who never knew defeat.
Thrown into prisons, for what I can't say,
neither could he if he was alive today.

His army wasn't the richest;
some members less than poor.
They believed in something called the spirit,
which is worth a lot more.

He predicted his future.
He said his time was near.
No one thought the general
would ever disappear.

But it happened in Memphis
on a warm spring night.
He walked out on a balcony
to see some sights.

A SHOT RANG OUT.
EVERYONE WAS STILL.
SOMEONE CRIED OUT,
"THE GENERAL HAS BEEN KILLED!"

Not a sound, not a word
was uttered that night,
for who would kill a general
in a NONVIOLENT fight?

As peace-loving as this general began,
he was even more peace-loving in the end.
Does the dream lie in dust?
Is it nothing but ash?

The general was killed
while fighting for the rights of many
who collected trash.

Kool Philly Earl

my man
lives near the corner of 5 – 2,
eats pork, drinks cheap wine

holds check in the Wissahickon Woods
City Hall, Broad, Market
and corners of lower land value

plays video games from 9 to 5
smokes pot, snorts coke

relieves himself in the ladies' room
blows his nose one nostril at time,
usually in the presence of women

has a room in the Y
but swims regularly at the art museum

under a hunter's moon
he will
prey in the alleys near 5 – 2
in empty subway cars
and underneath city hall

in the early morning hours
trolley cars tow him home

God, he loves this city.

1622 Virginia Massacre

Opechancanough, a Powhatan chief,
awoke early one morning
and sent his braves to fight.

He said, "Butcher all of the
European settlers
and destroy all desecrating sights."

For one hundred and forty-five miles,
the Powhatans' howls
awakened the settlers to death.

After killing three hundred and forty-seven settlers,
the Powhatans obediently left.

If the Powhatan Indians had been successful
in carrying out Opechancanough's notion,
there wouldn't have been one settler left alive
and survivors would have drowned in the **OCEAN.**

The survivors retreated to Jamestown colony,
located in Virginia
I was told.
Settlers communicated to others
what the Powhatans had done
and to **all Natives,** the settlers became cold.

Ain't Gonna Be No Revolution

You can stop that lie.
You can't watch your boy get zapped.
You can't watch your mother die.
It might be a little bloodshed
about a pint or two,
but the only blood that you'll shed
will be that five-dollar pint
to cop some drugs for you...

You can't fool me,
talking all that bull,
breath smelling like wine,
begging true sisters and brothers
for nickels and dimes.

Ain't gonna be no revolution;
stop telling that lie.
Where was the revolution?
You watched
Medgar, Malcolm, and Martin **die!**
Where were you and your boys?
You heard the shots.
Don't pretend you **forgot!**
Ain't   gonna   be   no   rev–o–lu–tion.

Who in the hell gave you the right
to predict a revolution in the future's sight?
Ain't gonna be no revolution, **BROTHER.**
Why should I hang up my mind on your lie?

Country vs City

"Say, man, look at that cat with the suede coat and the suede shoes."

"Man, that's Carl. Me and him went to the same school.
He wore army clothes and burlap bags for shoes.
Now check out his walk, all calm and kool,
trying to fool us like he's a city dude.
Hey, Carl, welcome back home."

"My name is Carlos, brother,
and this place I wouldn't own.
I'm from Philly, brother, the city of love."

"Ah, come on, Carl. Cut out that jive.
I've been kicking your ass since you were five."

With a flick of his wrist and a flash of his blade,
Carl thought with a bluff he had the country dude
made.
Carl closed his blade and said, "Ah man,
that was just for fun."
The city dude
 had drawn a gun.
"See there? I told you, man;
you don't know nothing about city life.
You still walking around with a damn knife."

Nam

it was called

reading a poem
about flowers
and trees waving in the wind
while the monsoon and napalm
send other pictures to my mind

remember the green grass in the park
cooking on the grills during holidays
playing in the grass
catch, softball, football, volleyball
chasing the younger kids
basketball on the courts

wild flowers blooming
birds singing
squirrels stealing food and chattering in the trees

we paid little or no attention too those things
didn't matter anyway
the napalm created other
permanent pictures
welcome home.

Fictitious Conceded Dodo

If I could afford
to pay my way around,
I wouldn't settle for
what I could get
but the best.
I wouldn't collect
March of Dimes,
pinch a coin or two,
sell chicken dinners on weekends,
or
stand in food lines.

If I could really pay my way around,
I wouldn't impersonate protégés
who are suave,
cool, and calm.
Advertise pantyhose, light beer,
or fast cars during TV commercials.

If I had the bread to pay my way around,
I wouldn't waste my time
keeping my mustache and hair groomed,
spending hours in the mirror
to
look like a movie star.
I can't pay my way around.
So, I don't pretend.
I'm not made of plastic,
and I am not a clown.

Silent Cause

Be passive, my brother, and bleed
while
confined in an unwise mental state.
Chained
by a bond of dependence.
Be passive, my brother, and bleed internally
when
Friday night rolls around.
Blow away your troubles.
Give a toast to the brothers
and bleed
while
wishing things were not the same.
Recalling
tip-of-the-tongue phenomena
about
war, Vietnam, and Purple Hearts
to
cite your heroic actions
for
sharing blood abroad
while
not knowing the cause.
You continue
to be
passive at home
but willingly
shed your blood
abroad.

West Africa

Fought my brother to become a free man.
Sold into slavery.
Shipped to a foreign land.

No Ellis Island or statue for me.
Just a constant struggle to become free…

Fought in wars and earned my stripes,
but   still
a struggle
to see light…

What is good
for
you
is not good for me.
Given a placebo,
but
now I can see
why fighting my brother will only enslave me.

Deep are the roots of this inherited tree.
Victory for some;
enslavement for me.

I once observed a dog walking inside
a chain-linked fence,
circling the yard, leaving urine-spotted scents.

The fence grew old,
was removed one day.
The dog continued to circle the
spot and stay.

Cold Love

A desire to be with someone
when there is no limit to your desires.

A moment to share and worship
a sentimental or metalogical thought
of listening to your heart.

Wanting to fondle or caress.
Not knowing your own feelings
and never revealing your true thoughts or emotions.

Unable to share with someone other than self
a feeling unknown,
evaluated by a sick soul,
as labeled to be, but not so.

No man or woman can challenge
the silence
of being in love,
so we accept the title of being cold.

Cold love is internal love
felt only by those who are in love with love.

For the man or woman who always asks,
answering the question is merely a task.

Existentialism

Individual freedom
and responsibility
negated through
conditioning.
America.
Utopianism.
Walden Two
people loving and living,
no moral
or   mental compass,
no materialistic plastics,
just
social psychology.
America.
Patriotic,   mechanical beings
being
trained
to
salivate
to
a   bell.
Freedom and
democracy
through others,   for others
Pavlov and Mendel.
The dog and pea.
Yin   and   yang.

Philosophical

and theoretical

data.

Bureaucracy.

DC.

Responsibilities negate

freedom,

love,

and individualism.

Poem

Contemplating haphazardly
time,
frequently blowing my mind.
Versions of mystical shadows
appearing, disappearing.
Flickers of flashing lights
beam across the forehead.
Zap.
Sometimes nothing,
others something.
Sirens, screams.
Critics gathering in a room,
analyzing the basis of a story or poem.
Blackness inside the mind.
Images being
shredded from the conscience upon the page.
Lying here,
waiting to continue the discharge,
watching others' mechanical movements.
A sentence fragment or phrase
incomplete, like the incoherence of this poem, story,
or page may be,
depending on the eye, mind, hand.
You, not me, the critic.

Laugh out loud; that's amusing.
Sit, stand, stare; pencils, pens, laptops.

Mind's eye evaluating the lucrative expressions
you hear, see, feel.

then discard them.
That's nice.
Mentally it doesn't move me.
Black men with white women
move you.
White men with Black women
move you.
A laxative overdose
will move you.
Inside the mind, bilingual pigments
mix freely, haphazardly
flowing from the stream of consciousness.

No Subject

Use rhymes to coincide
with the eyes and mind.
Iambic pentameter,
romantic mechanics.
Hopkins, Wordsworth, Keats.
Electrifying sprung rhythm
Lyrical ballads.
A dream, not a scheme.
Continue the process;
regress a mess.
Synthesizing sounds,
syllogisms,
psychological,
philosophical,
both
blind in mind.
Iambic rhymes,
not times.

Survival

the wind howls
trees stand tall
while portable houses roll aimlessly by.
Complete, incomplete,
unstable, roaming freely

carpet rows of leaves on trees
shed their multiple colors.
bluish gray skies suggest
 physical or mental change

the road ahead seems long;
rough mountain peaks ahead

no change for the portable houses
with concrete foundations;
it will roll along instead.

Set Me Free

Don't bury me on the side of a hill.
Water runs in my casket,
           make my eyes tear.
Don't bury me under a tree.
Shade in the winter
           too cold for me.
Don't bury me near a busy road.
People will pass who
           I don't know.
Don't bury me in an open field.
The wind and snow
           will make me chill.
Don't bury me in the cold, cold ground.
Can't hear what's above,
           moving around.
Don't bury me in a mausoleum.
No rich soil
           to support gynoeciums.
Bury my shell where thou please.
Take my spirit
where there are <u>thee.</u>

Bougie

Get down.
Syllogistic sounds; symbolism
up down.
waves of an ocean
played from   sheet music
slide   trombone
in out.
Valves torpedoing into
cubby holes,   producing
high tides.
Get down.
Metaphorical   mounds
pitcher's   first round
no hits, no runs
two left
tango   both mounds   dig the sounds
Get down.
It takes one hit to get on
two mounds.
A good slide trombone
and precise fingering of valves to get down.

Xmas Poem

Here we are
together again,
watching snowflakes fall
 heavier this time,
falling past the window,
reminding me of Xmas.
But,
 something much warmer
than
sitting by a fireplace,
watching chestnuts roasting on an open fire
or
Jack Frost
 nipping at noses.
A fantasy world
with thrills, chills, periodic gay laughter.
Silvery silence,
heavy breathing,
children sleeping?
Eyes closed and opened wide,
waiting for Santa
to
slide into that narrow chimney with his
big
bag
of
 toys.

"Santa will come
whether it snows or not."

Love and Lovers

Love is giving more of yourself to someone
who really doesn't love you.

It's a devotion of your time
and a sacrifice of your pleasures
for someone who really doesn't care.

It's the duty of the loved or lover
to understand one another.

Understanding is truly a trial of love.
Without understanding, there is no love.

Love is unhappiness one feels
when a lover has gone astray.
It's the emptiness that one feels
when a lover has gone away.

Love is anything that makes your heart
burn with pain,
your eyes flow like rain.

Is it true that love "makes the world go round"?

If there is no love
The world would truly not be...

Coinage

Mental Block—
can't get your gitty on

like trying to get started
get interrupted and stop;
like trying to complete
a thought
get a mental block

you can't get your gitty on

like waking up early,
trying to get a blow;
nothing in the kitchen but spaghetti,
yo!

you can't get your gitty on

no jam for the bread.
no bacon with the eggs.
kids in your bed,
start watching the clock.
get a mental block

you can't get your gitty on.
like trying to visit a friend
cross-town
traffic stop and go;
lights,

changing slow.
cars weaving in/out
"damn cell phones in their mouth"
in-laws
at your friend's house

you can't get your gitty on

like watching pedestrians,

cross the street slow,
rears rhythmically moving
like dance-hall lights.
some are **P-H-A-T;**
others need to cut that shit out.

GITTY'S UP!

there's eye candy.
you abruptly stop,
get rear-ended,
get a mental block.
can't get your gitty on.

Company Man

I'm there early
to
set the clock,
late in the evenings
to
close and lock.

I keep subordinates

                             in their place
with lies, half truths,
and   sometimes,   mace.

I keep my brethren
working hard in their fields
with promises of promotions,
false hope,
and   pretentious   goodwill.

I can speak the language of Shakespeare
to
brag or boast
"To be or not to be…"

                    there's no doubt
at 5:00 p.m.,   I'm punching out.

I'll snitch to the big boss
if you come in early,

early quit,
or come late.

take credit
for
your hard work
if you stay past eight.

There are no illusions
about my status quo.
I'll keep treating you bad;
you'll keep asking for mo.

I'll keep you bending
'til you break.
I'll feed you pork chops;
you'll think it's steak.

I'll make you cry,
weep, and moan;
you'll beg for more work,
and I will send you home.

Don't hallucinate about me,
Mother…
Tick me off?
I'll call your significant
other.

Let them know how you
procrastinate
and took your coworker

out on a date.

Don't fool with me.
Everyone know
just before the holiday,
I'll let you go.

If you have any doubt
about my position,
I have keen eyesight
and a strong intuition.

Blue Family

Blue family in my house,
can't get them out.

Turned off the heat,
gas,
electric,
water, and air;
visited a friend for four weeks;
came back;
 they were still there.

Blues in my house;
 can't get them out.

Called my therapist to help me through.
She asked, "Is this about the Blues?
I need help with them too."

First of the month,
they left to cash their government checks.
I put shutters on the windows,
changed all of the locks
before they got back,
laid my head on my pillow to take a brief rest.

I heard someone say, "Don't move. You are under arrest."
I said, "What the hell…"

Then, I heard the Blue family member say,

"Yes, Officer. He kicked in the door this time.
I don't know what's wrong with him.
I think he's got a messed-up mind."

They Mirandized me.
I said, "What the hell?
The cops said, "Shut up, crazy fool."
Blues said, "Cuff him.
Take his ass to jail."

Part II - Blues

Blues are in my house,
can't get them out.

Officers said, "You have one phone call for your lawyer or bail.
Otherwise, sit your ass right here in jail."

My lawyer caught a case.
Can't give him a call.
Blues are responsible for him taking a fall.

Called all of my siblings to bail me out.
They asked, "Are the Blues still in your house?"
They said, "Sorry, bro, we can't help you out.
You got the Blues in your house.
Once you let them in, you can never get them out."

I said, "Please, Officer, let me make one more call.
I know the Blues have a cell.
They all drive Escalades and hogs."

"Collect call for the Blues."
"Hello."
"Hey, Cousin Blue.
You know I'm in jail?"
"Hell, yeah, I know.
We put you there."

"Come on, Blue;
you're in my house.
Have some pity and bail me out."

"You changed the locks
and put shutters on the house.
WHY IN THE HELL
SHOULD WE BAIL YOU OUT?"

Arraigned in court, thought I had the case beat for a minute.
Then the Blues began to talk...
I was shackled,
handcuffed,
masked,
restrained in a chair,
sent to solitary confinement
when the Blues finished in there.
Lord have mercy.

"Don't ever let the Blues in your house."
Once you let them in,
you can never get them out..."

Snitches Get Stitches

Baby girl and baby boy
playing games   and riding bikes
in front of their house.

Mom and Dad inside,
chilling out.
TV news report, *"Over 300 shot dead."*
Family members
just scratch their heads
while rappers tout,
"Snitches get stitches."

Snitches get stitches.
My brother and sister
were robbed in broad daylight
among a crowd of people.
They all took flight

while moms and dads
were chilling in the house,
 listening to the rappers tout,
"Snitches get stitches."

You know,
it's a shame that child was killed
for his jersey, shoes, and bike,
while moms and dads
were chilling in the house,

listening to the rappers tout,
"Snitches get stitches."
Yes.
Snitches get stitches.

Baby's momma missing several months,
found dead,
pregnant,
bullet in her head...

Were you anywhere near the grassy knoll?
Only took one bullet to silence his soul.
One bullet in the head
heard around the world.

There were no snitches.
No one received stitches.

Can we solve these problems with community relations
or move to the suburbs
and wait for home invasions?

Baby girl and baby boy
playing games and riding bikes
in front of their house.
Suddenly,
shots rang out!

"OH LORD, NOT THE BABIES!"
I heard someone shout!

Baby girl and baby boy both snuffed out
while moms and dads were chilling in the house.
A whole generation
gunned down in the streets jailed, drugged, self-defeat.

While hailed in high praise
that SNITCHES GET STITCHES
even sung in songs
lined   pockets
with riches.

Babies, brothers, sisters, mommas,
JFK near the grassy knoll
would be alive today
had someone told.

One generation is lost,
another generation dying

socialization and communication is dead.

No one left to snitch.
No one left to stitch.

Go ahead, snitches; take your stitches.
The next bullet
may be aimed at your head.

Bow-Wow

wanna be your dog
stay from dusk to dawn
all day long
 till daylight is gone

take you to my home
work on you all night long
start over at dawn
put some coffee on

wanna be your dog
walk with you all day long
turn your lights off and on
fetch, growl, and groan
keep things from going on
protect your house and home
keep your budget strong

now your dog has gone
leash was too long
was carrying his own
you want him back home
took his old bone
the dog is gone

Boulevard Traffic

She appeared to be optimistic
a little different
 7:30 a.m.
decked out in red
77 degrees
windy
raining
trees and she
moving in rhythm
as if listening to a bootleg copy
of Miles'
Kind of Blue
bending forward occasionally,
adjusting her boobs,
peering down the boulevard
for a bus or date
GSA had to have an impact
camera flash
caught a glimpse
of
someone wearing
a pink backpack
a hat with feathers on both sides
earrings in both ears
So what?

Writing Group Prompt

COLLATERAL DAMAGE BY NO INTENTION
not sure what that mean
being a 'Nam vet I should.
remember sharing
but
not being part of the group
collateral damage
and isolation

"TRACTOR CROSSING," the sign read
picture of a farmer sitting on a tractor wearing a straw hat
no fields, barns, cows, horses, chickens, or people
no other farm equipment

only a farmer sitting on a tractor, wearing a straw hat
similar to the hats Vietnamese farmers and civilians wore;
no other symbols, signs,
feelings, or respect

for the body count
isolated like the farmer
or the wounded vet
following a prompt,
sensing a nonverbal cross
collateral damage.

Taking Off to Parts Unknown

Retirement,
let's see.
Hang out with friends.
High blood pressure, low blood pressure, diabetes, arthritis
too old, tired

travel
not enough money
wear and tear on the body

develop a bucket list
what size bucket
medical appointments
thirty-sixty,   ninety-day
wait
just do what you feel
blame it on being old
or being you.

Inside the Zone

I sat on the side of a road.

Not sure where.

Vietnam

maybe,

or

was I home?

Still trying to figure that out;

trying to find that connection

with

family, friends, others,

in my mind

in my home

and in my zone.

All of the Time in the World

The other day I was thinking about some friends I grew up with
and all of the fun we had

playing sports, games, school, dates, dances, church.

I couldn't remember everyone's name.

Too much time passed, I guess.

A couple of months ago I visited the Wall in DC.

When I approached, I began to recognize the names of friends,

even those I had forgotten.

My mind went back to our youth and thinking that we had all of
the time in the world.

Thoughts

Teach your children the wrong things.

They will still be blessed by God

A positive effect of being exposed to negative trauma

A person who self-medicates may use drugs and alcohol.

A person who has prescribed meds may use drugs and alcohol as well.

Some people work for God

Some people do God's work

Who are you?

Almost Spring

March 2018

the snow keeps falling
trickling down
through the pores in my helmet
down to the amygdala

sun shines for a brief while
flowers keep blooming
not knowing the dangers
that may unfold

snowing again,
it's cold and wet;
i don my combat gear and poncho
to protect me from the elements
then began walking
to stay warm

the flowers followed their own instincts
bloomed early, thinking it was spring,
now buried under the snow

when i arrived home i followed my instincts—
braved the elements without my poncho or combat gear,
thinking
it was *Almost Spring.*

American Dream

Soldat
in America
drinks a 40 before breakfast,
takes prescribed meds
smokes pot
snorts coke to take off the edge.

Grew up on the corners of 5 – 2 in Philly.
Seen often near the wood lines of Bucks County
and the Wissahickon Creek.

Frequents Broad and Market,
the Boulevard,
Mills Mall,
local convenience stores
in Bucks County,
and occasionally spotted
at
Neshaminy or Oxford Valley Malls
with palms up.

His physical appearance
reflects a need for support.

The visible internal scars
and slight limp
accentuate
his distinguished service
and his inability to mold himself into society.

Poetic City Funk

Long blocks of cement,
concrete and steel,
hot and muggy in the summer.
Cold to the bone in the winter

Communities of isolated individuals
 living on a cement block;
some because of cultures,
others on their own.

Those who have
and the have-nots

Economics plays a key role in creating dividing lines
between
those who live on the concrete blocks
 those who live elsewhere
and others who choose to live on their own
the haves and the have nots

One of the most depressing things in the city is not being
connected
to the haves or the have-nots.
You find yourself isolated
sitting on a porch, step, or stoop
Self-medication can be an exit out
or a deeper entrance within.

One may think the question,

"What games must I learn to play in order not to be amiss?"

I must admit that the word sounds good,

but so does banjo,

and neither one will fit

in this urban abyss

I can write and write and write and write…

but what will it mean?

I have many soul mates on this urban block,

but very few will share my soul.

There are many who will connect the lines and phrases

to say what is written here,

 but only a few will tap into the creative flow.

I think writers write to write like singers sing to sing.

Words that are sung are a little different from words that are written

but the same.

Both are a mental rhythm of the mind

created from

the hot, muggy summers

bone-chilling winters, isolation, and the steel and concrete that bind

Made in the USA
Coppell, TX
20 August 2021

60728992R00035